Edinburgh

Scotland's Capital

A compact city with centuries of history,
Edinburgh's centre can be toured in one day,
although that would be doing it an injustice. Simply
exploring the magnificent castle could take over half
a day and the Royal Mile is equally as intriguing at
night as during the day. This book graphically
portrays the scenes that make Edinburgh one of the
most beautiful cities in the world.

Photography by
Graeme Wallace

Edinburgh
Scotland's Capital

INTRODUCTION

Scotland's capital since the 15th century, Edinburgh is a city of contrast crying out to be explored. From the outset you cannot fail to recognise the wealth of historical buildings from the magnificent castle lording over the capital atop its volcanic mound, through to the soaring Scott Monument and down to the Palace of Holyroodhouse. Upon closer investigation there is a second aspect to Edinburgh hidden behind the main street of the Royal Mile. Accessed via the passageways or closes and wynds, most of the early 15th and 16th century terraced dwellings had to make way for the multi-storied tenement schemes erected during the 17th century to accommodate the capital's over-crowding problem. Wealthy merchants also took advantage of building homes down these closes and off the filthy main thoroughfare. Perhaps the best glimpse back to old Edinburgh and its cramped, claustrophobic conditions is Mary King's Close. Sealed off and forgotten for centuries, this is one of four closes hidden below the City Chambers that was literally built on top of them in 1753. A stark reminder of the squalid and unhygienic environment in which people lived. Sickness and diseases including the great plague of 1645, resulted in an early death for many of the inhabitants who dwelt in these streets.

Lawnmarket, Canongate and the Grassmarket still give an indication of the hard life people endured during the16th and 17th centuries. Look above the brightly painted shop fronts and facades to see the gabled ended roofs and soaring buildings of a bygone era. The great many public houses provided an escape from the squalor and today act as mini museums with their tales of local history.

Following the creation of the United Kingdom in 1707 a period of peace, confidence and prosperity began. In stark contrast to the overcrowded old city and in conjunction with the erection of the North Bridge across Nor Loch in 1772, the "New Town" was underway. Bold fashionable properties along the broad promenade of George Street and beyond reflect a period of wealth and celebration. From the grand building now the headquarters for the Royal Bank of Scotland at the eastern end to the epitome of practical Georgian design with Charlotte Square at the opposite end; this is the best-preserved example of a Georgian town-planning in Europe. Simultaneously, Calton Hill was chosen as the site for a random selection of monuments that were erected between the late 18th to the mid 19th century.

The two towns are divided by Princes Street Gardens; an area that was once a Loch into which the old city's refuse was dumped and which is now a peaceful and beautifully landscaped garden. Scattered with monuments, the gardens including 19th century neo-classical and gothic masterpieces such as the Scott Monument, the National Gallery and the Royal Scottish Academy.

Finally, not content with dozens of fine buildings portraying the 16th through to the 19th century, Edinburgh also has several bold and striking buildings reflecting 20th century architecture and now boasts the new Scottish Parliament building as a statement of 21st century design.

ACKNOWLEDGMENTS

Photography by **Graeme Wallace**
Designed by **Kevin Jeffery**
Reprographics by **GWP Graphics**
Printed by **Printer Trento, Italy**

Published by
GW Publishing
PO Box 6091, Thatcham, Berks, RG19 8XZ.
Tel: +44 (0)1635 268080

Edinburgh is steeped in mystery, history and culture.
Photographer Graeme Wallace has walked the capital's streets
and climbed the surrounding hills countless times in order to
capture the city's character. Often working from early
morning until late evening to catch the atmospheric mood
created by the rising and setting sun, Graeme has endeavored
to portray Scotland's capital as the thriving historical city for
which it is famed.

Pictured above, Dougald Stewart Monument
Pictured opposite, Edinburgh from Arthur's Seat
Pictured page 1, Scottish Piper on Calton Hill
Pictured page 2, Edinburgh Castle
Pictured page 4, Edinburgh City
Front Cover, Edinburgh Castle
Back Cover, Edinburgh Military Tattoo
Inside Front Cover, Wallace Dress Tartan
Inside Back Cover, Wallace Hunting Tartan

Edinburgh
Scotland's Capital

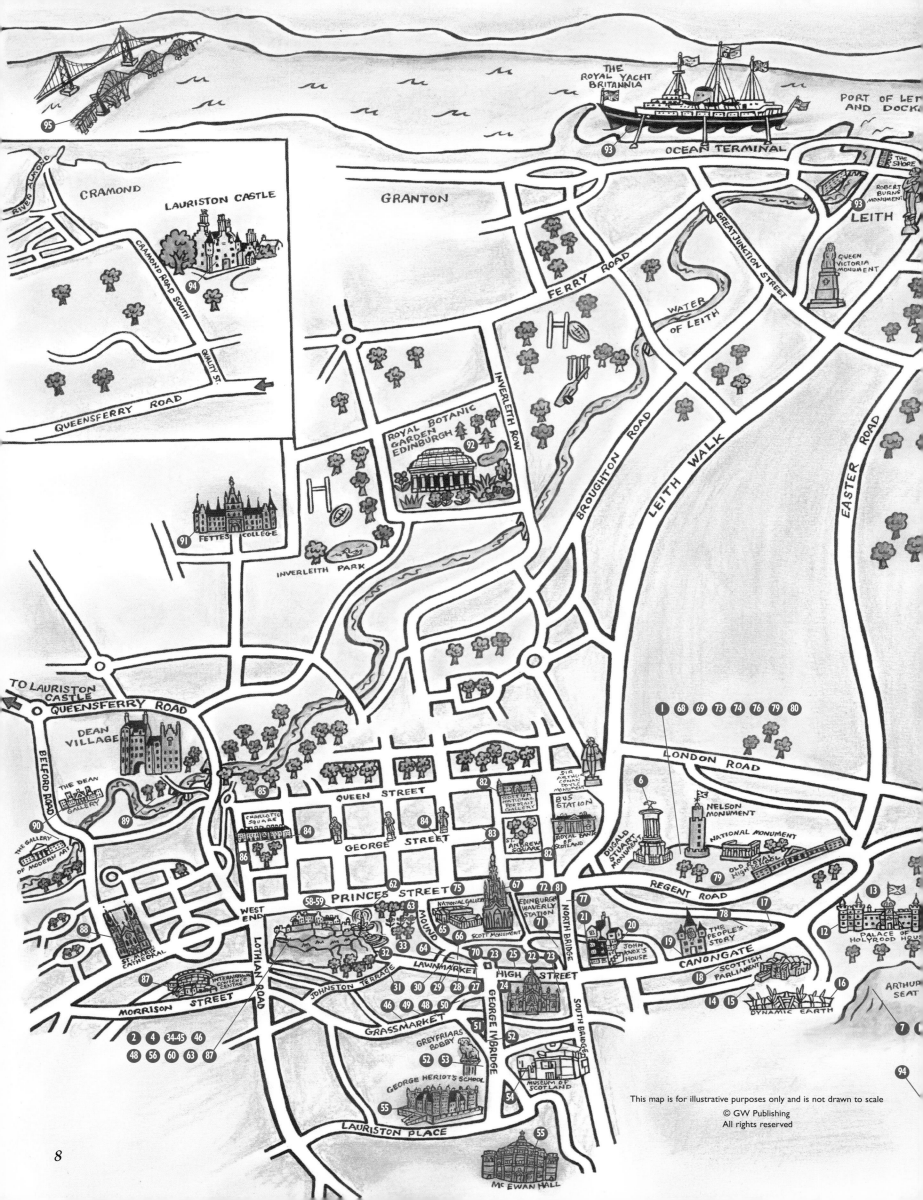

This map is for illustrative purposes only and is not drawn to scale

8

Edinburgh

Scotland's Capital

Contents

The Old Town -
East to West

The 'Old Town' of Edinburgh largely comprises of the Royal Mile; a sequence of five adjoining streets including Abbey Strand, Canongate, High Street, Lawnmarket and Castle Hill that run from the Palace of Holyroodhouse all the way up to the crag on which the Castle stands. Running parallel to the Royal Mile the Old Town also incorporated the Cowgate and the area known as the Grassmarket, directly below the castle.

Despite the passing of 800 years, it is not hard to appreciate how people lived in the medieval city. The vast number of narrow and sometimes eerie wynds and closes lead to the hidden city within.

View of Edinburgh Castle from Arthur's Seat

Edinburgh is a city built on seven hills, the highest of these being Arthur's Seat 251m (823ft) situated at the foot of the old city. A dormant volcano, it provides the perfect vantage point to view the old town from Holyrood Park all the way up to the Castle, then across to Leith, the Firth of Forth and beyond to the Kingdom of Fife.

Palace of Holyroodhouse

Just below Arthur's Seat, the Palace of Holyroodhouse is the official Scottish residence of Her Majesty The Queen Elizabeth II. Situated at the eastern end of the Royal Mile it was originally a guesthouse for the early kings. The baronial palace dating back to 1501 is best known as being the residence of Mary Queen of Scots and for the infamous

murder in 1566 of her secretary, Rizzio who was stabbed 56 times by her jealous husband and companions.

Mary's claim to the throne of England and her staunch catholic beliefs led to her troubled life ending in her being beheaded by her cousin, Elizabeth I. For all her troubles, Mary's son James VI of Scotland did succeed his mother's ambitions to become James I of England.

Holyrood Abbey

Established in 1128 by King David 1, following his miraculous escape while out hunting, from an enraged stag which reportedly had a cross or rood between its antlers. Upon grabbing the rood, the animal retreated resulting in the founding and naming of Holy Rood Abbey.

Queen Mary's Bath House

Just beyond the Palace of Holyroodhouse, this tiny building was probably a pavilion or lodge. The small cavity in the wall of the early 17th century property is reputed to have contained a bath although it is more likely that it was a simple hiding place in times of danger.

Abbey Strand

The canons of Holyrood Abbey were permitted to build homes just outside the gate of their abbey. Consequently many grand properties were constructed during the 12th century in the area to become known as the Canongate.

Scottish Parliament Building

Commissioned on behalf of the reconvened Scottish parliament in 1998 by Donald Dewar, the building was designed by architect, Enric Miralles. Considered his greatest achievement the ambitious building is cloaked in many 'secrets'! Perhaps best viewed from Arthur's Seat, the parliament reveals a 'fifth' facade.

Designed to engage the imagination, one is left to ponder whether the structure with its glistening fanned stainless steel roof represent leaves, upturned boats, pebbles or perhaps silver fish? What is not left to any doubt is the craftsmanship, attention to detail and beautiful use of modern and traditional materials from oak, sycamore, granite to stainless-steel and concrete.

MSP Building

A mosaic series of pre-cast concrete units, each of the stainless-steel windows represents an MSP's office, described by architect Enric Miralles as 'contemplative spaces' or 'think pods'

Whitehorse Close

Dating from the 16th century as the Royal Mews and named after Queen Anne's white palfrey, Whitehorse Close was originally an inn and coaching stable. Totally remodelled in 1889 it subsequently provided accommodation for lower paid workers. However the close was modernised again in 1962 making it one of the brightest closes along the Royal Mile.

Our Dynamic Earth

Overshadowed by the Salisbury Crags, Scotland's tented roofed millennial attraction offers a 'dynamic' insight into 4,500 years of geographical and natural history.

Huntly House

Now part of the Museum of Edinburgh, Huntly House was built in 1570 and is believed to have been the hunting lodge of George, sixth Earl and first Marquiss of Huntly. Rebuilt with stone, it appears to have originally been a timber structure.

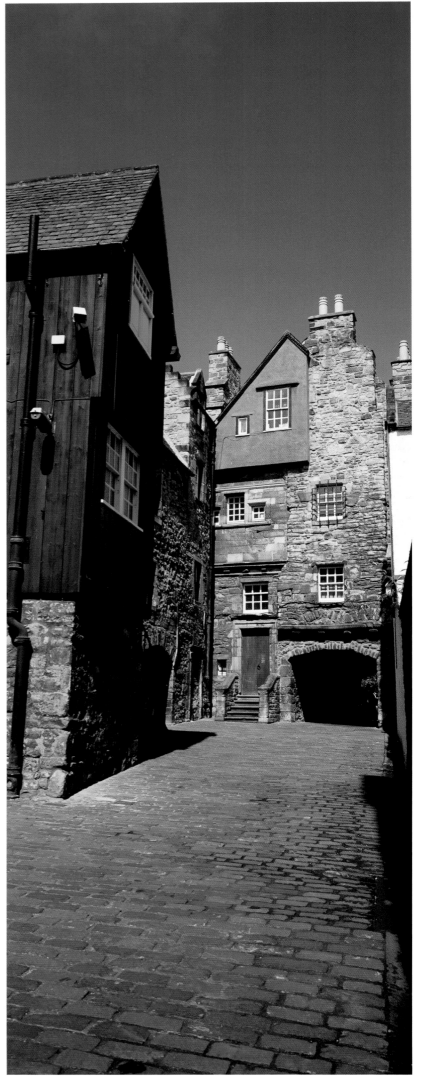

Museum of Edinburgh

An excellent museum doing much to captivate the imagination, showing Canongate as it was in bygone eras.

Tenement Housing,
189 Canongate

A typical tenement building restored in 1954 to closely resemble its 17th century appearance.

Tolbooth, The People's Story

Rebuilt in 1591, this prominent building with its protruding clock was once the tolbooth for the Canongate district and has served as a council chamber, tax point, prison, fire station and now a museum telling the social story of the 'ordinary' people who once lived in these streets.

John Knox House

Part of this building has been dated back to 1420 although the frontage was added in the early 16th century. With its prominent corner position, jutting out onto the narrow street, the house was considered 'ruinous' and an 'encumbrance' resulting in it being destined to be pulled down. Fortunately it was spared demolition by the efforts of John Knox who is believed to have lived and died here in 1572. Remarkably, it now stands as the only remaining example of a townhouse in Edinburgh with exposed timber galleries.

Moubray House

Built as housing by Andrew Moubray in 1529, the little shop and frontage were added in the 19th century. Once the home of Daniel Defoe, author of 'Robinson Crusoe' the property extends several blocks back from its picturesque frontage.

21

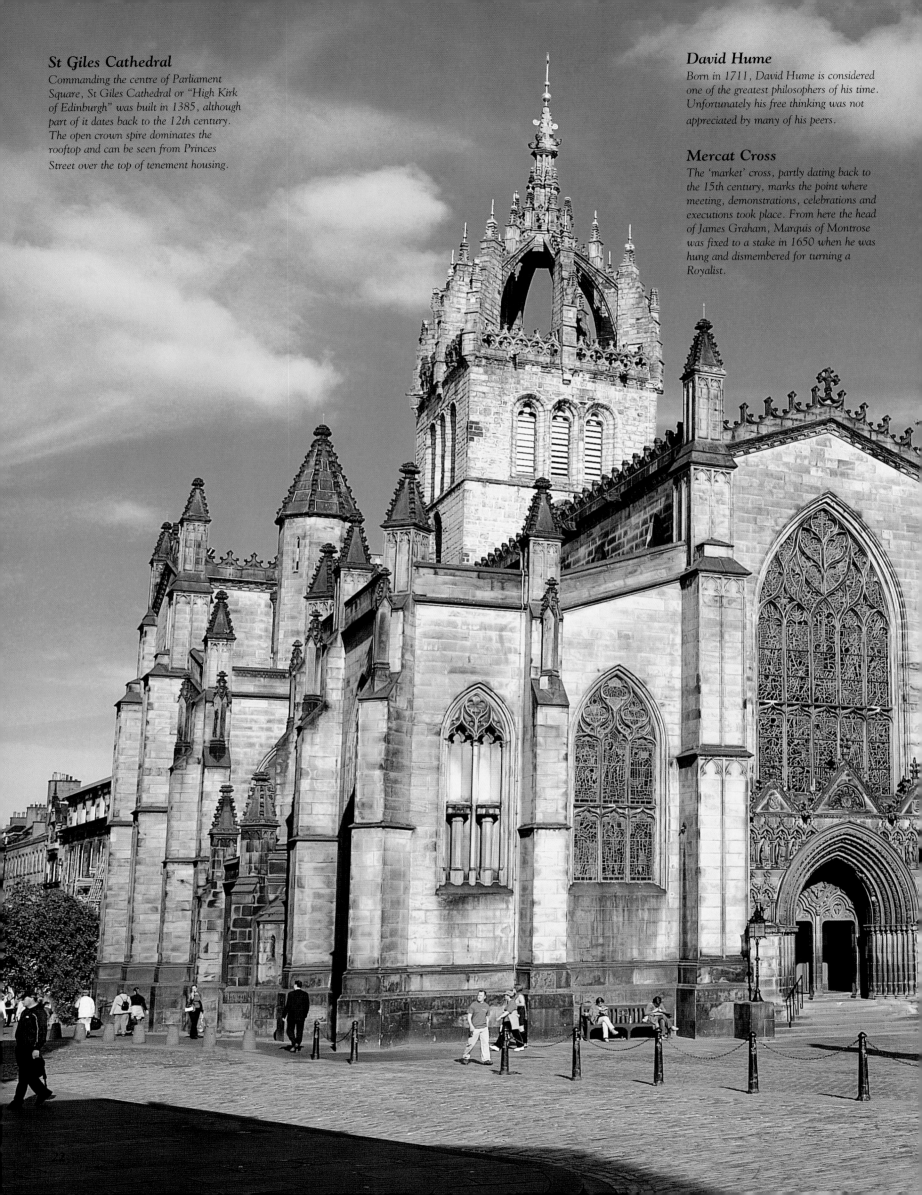

St Giles Cathedral

Commanding the centre of Parliament Square, St Giles Cathedral or "High Kirk of Edinburgh" was built in 1385, although part of it dates back to the 12th century. The open crown spire dominates the rooftop and can be seen from Princes Street over the top of tenement housing.

David Hume

Born in 1711, David Hume is considered one of the greatest philosophers of his time. Unfortunately his free thinking was not appreciated by many of his peers.

Mercat Cross

The 'market' cross, partly dating back to the 15th century, marks the point where meeting, demonstrations, celebrations and executions took place. From here the head of James Graham, Marquis of Montrose was fixed to a stake in 1650 when he was hung and dismembered for turning a Royalist.

Edinburgh Fringe Festival

Despite its title 'Fringe' Festival this two week event with over 1,000 shows performed in hundreds of venues is the biggest Arts festival in the world and dates back over 50 years.

Juggling is a popular form of street entertainment during the Fringe Festival, although juggling with knives and chain saws is not the norm!

The theatrical costumes spill out onto the streets as performers patiently wait for your money before doing a turn. With meticulous attention to detail it is sometime tricky to differentiate between real and illusion.

Advocates Close

Considered to shelter one of Edinburgh's oldest house dating from the mid 15th century. Advocates Close was considered a pretty close enhanced by the terraced gardens and the view across Princes Street Gardens to the Scott Monument.

Lawnmarket

One of the oldest streets in Scotland and once a hive of activity as the city's cloth market place, the Lawnmarket epitomises Edinburgh's population crisis with soaring tenement housing towering over either side of the street and beyond as wynds or alleyways were created to allow even more tenements to be erected.

Deacon Brodie's Tavern

This attractive public house or tavern is named after the infamous William Brodie who became the inspiration for Robert Louis Stevenson's novel 'Jekyll and Hyde'. A respected figure Brodie was a town councillor and deacon of the Edinburgh Wrights and Masons guild. However by night his character changed as he became a womaniser, gambler and thief. He was eventually convicted a hanged in 1788.

Blackie House,
Wardrop's Close

ABOVE *Passageways lead to the two closes,
Wardrop's and Lady Stair's which form an
open courtyard surrounded by steeply
rising facades on all four sides. Despite the
squalor the poor children of the close-knit
communities of Blackie House and
adjoining properties could play here safe
from the busy main street.*

The Writers' Museum,
Lady Stair's Close

BELOW *Hidden from the main street and
adjacent to Blackie House is the 17th
century mock-Jacobean merchant's home,
Lady Stair's House - a much more
accommodating property. As Robert
Burns lived to the east of the close in 1786
the house is now The Writers' Museum, a
fitting place to commemorate the work of
Scotland's most renowned literary figures.*

Gladstone's Land

LEFT *Rebuilt in the 17th century, Gladstone's Land (or housing block) is the only property in Edinburgh that still has an arcaded front, a development of the timber galleries which protruded over the street.*

The Deacon's House

ABOVE *The home of Deacon Brodie's father, the 15th century arched kitchen was Brodie's cabinet-making workshop.*

Milne's Court

Built by James Mylne, the King's Master Mason in 1690, the buildings surrounding Milne's Court are the earliest examples of the post-Revolution housing schemes, designed to address the stifling poverty and gruelling streets.

Tolbooth Church

At 73m (240ft) the soot blackened spire of the old Tolbooth Church soars higher than any other spire in Edinburgh and is clearly visible from all directions.

Camera Obscura

The white and black tower atop this 17th century building is in fact a periscope allowing 360' views of Edinburgh through a series of mirrors and lenses. The Obscura also has a large-scale pinhole camera as well as other 'obscure' optical tricks. The roof top offers great views of the Royal Mile and inside Milne's Court.

Ramsay Garden

Commenced in 1854 these attractive 'student quarters' were built around the homes of poet Allan Ramsay and his son Allan Ramsay the painter. Due to their location they now command some of the highest property prices in Edinburgh.

Edinburgh Castle Esplanade

The Celts from 600AD are the earliest people believed to have recognised the strategic importance of the site on which the castle now stands. Shortly thereafter, it was fortified by the conquering Northumbrians from just south of the border. After 400 years the rock was back in Scots' hands with Malcolm III building a hunting lodge on the site. The gatehouse was added in 1888, with the bronze statues of Sir William Wallace and King Robert the Bruce as sentries either side being the most recent addition to the castle, added in 1926.

St Margaret's Chapel, Edinburgh Castle

David I, son of Malcolm III built the chapel and dedicated it to his mother, Queen Margaret. It remains as the oldest part of the castle and the oldest building in Edinburgh, dating the castle back to c1250.

Argyle Battery, Edinburgh Castle

The six-gun Argyle Battery defended the north side of the castle and offers superb views of Princes Street Gardens, the New Town and beyond.

Foogs Gate & The Scottish National War Memorial, Edinburgh Castle

Foog's Gate was the main entry to the Upper Ward and was built in the 17th century. The castle church of St Mary's once stood at the north side of Crown Square, it was eventually demolished and replaced by the building which is now the Scottish National War Memorial, converted to it's current use in 1927.

Mons Meg,
Edinburgh Castle

*Presented to James II in 1457 and with
the capacity to propel a 150kg (330lb)
cannonball over 3km (2 miles), Mons
Meg is one of the two largest siege guns
ever built, and surprisingly weighing 6 tons
was transported across Scotland for that
very purpose to devastating effect.
However it took 100 men to move it 5km
(3 miles) per day and was subsequently
taken out of service in 1540.*

The Edinburgh Military
Tattoo

*The Edinburgh Military Tattoo has been
running for over 50 years with
performances from British and
international military forces, the highlight
being the Massed Pipes and Drums.*

The Queen's Colour
Squadron of the Royal Air
Force (Left)

Club Piruett (Right)

The Military Band of The
People's Liberation Army of
China (Below Right)

The Massed Highland
Dancers (Below)

**1st Battalion The Royal
Highland Fusiliers**

**Band Leader of The Cape
Town Highlanders**

**Band Leader of The
Dragoon Guards**

Grassmarket

For almost 500 years, the Grassmarket held a weekly livestock market. Street traders still use it today to sell from their stalls although the sale of livestock here is a thing of the past.

Edinburgh Castle
from the Grassmarket

Towering above the four story homes, bars and pavement cafes of Grassmarket, the castle dominates the city all around it. The prominent aspect of the castle is the Great Hall, below which are the prison vaults which once incarcerated over 500 French prisoners during the mid 18th century and again in the 1793-1815 Napoleonic war.

Edinburgh Castle
from Johnston Terrace

Protecting the Royal Palace which stands behind it, the circular Half Moon Battery was built in 1573 on top of the 14th century, David's Tower that was destroyed in the great siege 1567-73.
Mary Queen of Scots gave birth to James V1 of Scotland in the Royal Palace in 1566. The honours of Scotland together with the Stone of Destiny are now displayed here.

The Last Drop, Grassmarket

RIGHT *Named after the frequent public hanging that took place just across the street, The Last Drop public house is built from rubble and is one of the oldest houses in Edinburgh.*

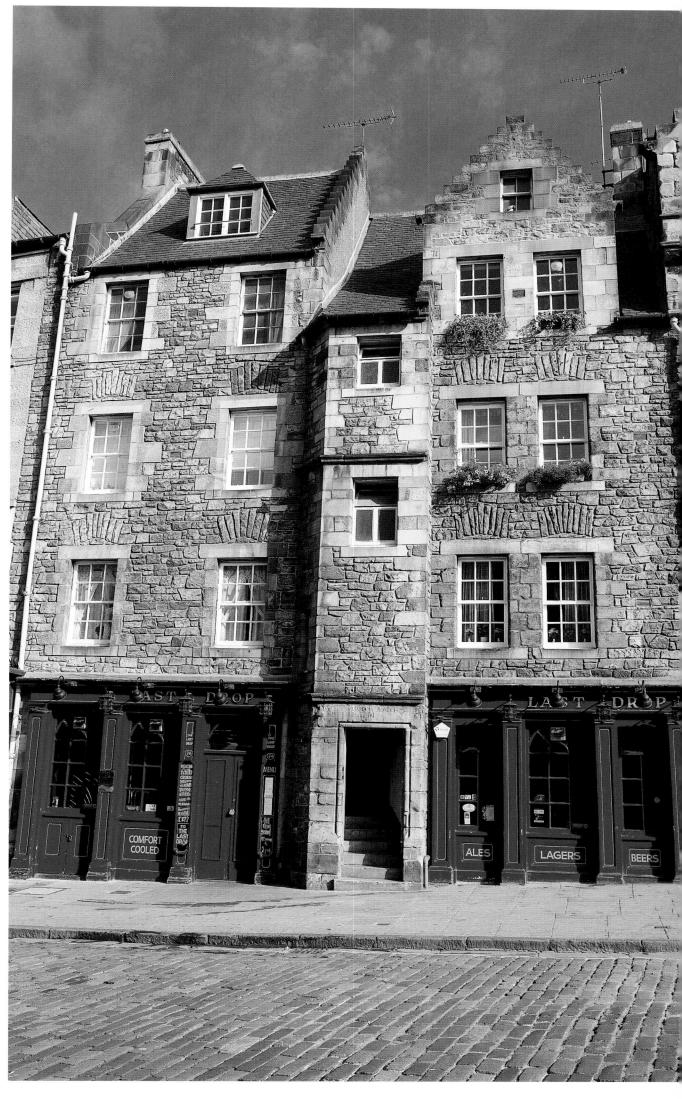

St Andrew's Cross, Grassmarket

LEFT *St Andrew's Cross marks the spot where the public gallows stood until 1784. Gallows that witnessed incredible activity in the 1660s with over 100 executions. Many were Covenanters who died for their beliefs during the recrimination or 'killing times' of Charles II as he tried to re-establish the Catholic faith.*

West Bow & Victoria Street

These two colourful streets abut at the point where the cobbled road bends as it rises up from the Grassmarket connecting to the Royal Mile.

Candlemaker Row

RIGHT *Candle making was a hazardous occupation with the melting tallow causing a workshop in Forrester's Wynd to catch fire in 1654. Consequently, the craftsmen were banished from the main thoroughfares and set up their shops and homes along the entirety of Candlemaker Row.*

Greyfriars Kirkyard

LEFT *Dating from 1620 but rebuilt in 1845 the unpretentious Greyfriars Kirk watches over as many as 80,000 graves including those of John Gray and his indisputably loyal dog, Bobby. The National Covenant was first signed here in 1638 and Cromwell's troops were barracked here in the 1650s.*

Tolbooth Church from Greyfriars Kirkyard

RIGHT *With dozens of once grand but now soot clad funeral monuments and tombstones alongside the foreboding compound where over 1000 Covenanters were held captive in 1672, many of them perishing through the freezing winter months, Greyfriars is claimed to be the eeriest graveyard in all of Scotland.*

Greyfriars Bobby

BELOW *Perhaps the most famous little dog in the world, Bobby, a Skye terrier, has been immortalised with his own life size bronze statue atop the water fountain. Loyal to his police owner, John Gray, even beyond his death in 1858, Bobby kept vigil over Gray's grave until his own death 14 years later.*

Museum of Scotland

ABOVE *Reminiscent of the round tower houses prevalent in many Scottish castles, the Museum of Scotland was built from pink and yellow sandstone in 1998 and is as bold and striking as many of the country's castles.*

McEwan Hall, University of Edinburgh

TOP RIGHT *Founded in 1582, the University of Edinburgh encompasses numerous buildings to the south of the city. The huge domed roofed McEwan Hall, part of the 'Old College', is used for ceremonial occasions.*

George Heriot's School

Goldsmith and jeweller at the Kings court, George Heriot bequeathed some of his wealth to establish this hospital school for orphan boys in 1628. In 1886 it became a boys' day school and is now a private school for both boys and girls.

Princes Street - West to East

Princes Street Gardens occupy the low-lying site of the Nor' Loch, constructed in the 15th century as part of the city's defences. The portion east of the Mound was drained to construct the foundations of North Bridge, while the unhealthy swamp immediately below the Castle was finally drained in 1820. Princes Street Gardens (first West, then, later, East) were laid out from 1816 onwards.

Edinburgh Castle - early morning
A defensive structure is likely to have held the castle mound since the Roman times of AD140.

Ross Fountain,
Princes Street Gardens

Thr Ross Fountain is a French cast iron sculpture made in Paris in 1862. Purchased in 1867 by Daniel Ross, an Edinburgh gunsmith it subsequently took its place below the castle in Princes Street Gardens in 1869.

West Princes Street Gardens

Once a defensive loch used for dumping the city waste, then a stinking pit that was drained from 1759 on, the gardens were created in 1816-20 as private gardens for people living on Princes Street and were opened to the public 60 years later. Now the centre to summer and winter festivals, climaxing at the end of the year with over 100,000 revellers bringing in the New Year.

Edinburgh Castle - at night

Even at night the castle's presence is indisputable.

Jazmundo

In the centre of West Princes Street Garden, bands take turns on the Ross Bandstand to give free public performances during the festival.

Clann An Drumma

*The sound of Clann An Drumma is
enough to make even the most battle
hardened soldier run in fear.*

War Memorial

ABOVE *An equestrian memorial erected by the Scots Greys after the South African War and later used to commemorate the regiment's dead in two world wars.*

Floral Clock

RIGHT *Recording the time for over 100 years, the Floral Clock is a functioning clock covered with over 20,000 small plants.*

Edinburgh Castle from Princes Street Garden

OPPOSITE *Perhaps the most famous view of Edinburgh Castle.*

Assembly Hall
and Ramsay Garden

Built as the New College of the Free
Church of Scotland in 1858, the
Assembly Building is still used as an
educational venue by the University of
Edinburgh and has been used as a debating
chamber by the new Scottish Parliament.
The unmistakable red roof of the adjacent
Ramsay Garden provided student
accommodation.

National Gallery of Scotland

A William Playfair masterpiece from
1854, it represents the classical Greek
revival of the time, helping Edinburgh
merit its title of 'The Athens of the
North'. It houses a collection of Scottish
art alongside works from Renaissance Italy
to the French Post-Impressionism period.

Royal Scottish Academy,
Assembly Hall and Tolbooth
Kirk

Bringing together the old and new town
architecture, the spire of Tolbooth Kirk
and the twin towers of the Assembly Hall
loom over the Royal Scottish Academy
building.

Old City Skyline

The late evening sun dramatically highlights the jagged skyline of the old city against the foreboding sky.

Scott Monument

Few monuments stand as tall or as striking as the gothic structure in honour of Sir Walter Scott. Commenced in 1840, just eight years after his death, the standing spire reveals the high esteem in which the Scots held their famous writer. 287 steps take you to the highest of four viewing platforms.

View of Calton Hill from Ramsay Garden

Stunning view to the north and east of Edinburgh can be enjoyed from the steep road above The Mound.

Calton Hill
from North Bridge

Acclaimed the 'Athens of the North', many of the monuments on Calton Hill were clearly inspired by classical Greek architecture.

Bank of Scotland
from North Bridge

The oldest bank in Scotland, established in 1695, The Bank of Scotland houses a small museum within its domed building atop The Mound.

The Scotsman Hotel

Built as part of the redevelopment of the North Bridge the building was designed for The Scotsman newspaper 1899-1904 and was the largest building to be erected by private enterprise in Edinburgh. It is now a hotel; The Scotsman newspaper having re-located to the eastern end of Holyrood Road, alongside the new Scottish Parliament buildings.

Balmoral Clock, Princes Street

Built by the North British Railway Company, the 5 star palatial Balmoral Hotel was built in 1902 and was originally known as the North British Station Hotel.

Nelson and National Monument, Calton Hill

Erected in honour of Admiral Lord Nelson's 1805 victory at the battle of Trafalgar, the Nelson Monument stands 32m (106ft) and resembles an upturned telescope. It took 8 years to build, being completed in 1815.

The building now known as the National Monument was actually intended as a church, replicating the Parthenon. Construction commenced in 1822 but funds ran out and it was never finished. Had it been completed, it would surely have been a magnificent icon holding a commanding position over the city.

Dugald Stewart Monument, Calton Hill

Worthy of any of Scotland's greatest achievers, the 1831 classical Greek colonnaded monument holds the prime position on Calton Hill and commemorates philosopher Dugald Stewart.

DUGALD STEWART
BORN NOVEMBER 22 1753
DIED JUNE 11 1828

Princes Street
from Calton Hill

The 'shopping street' Princes Street is also
the centre for Hogmanay celebrations.

Calton Hill from Arthur's Seat.

Just below the monuments on Calton Hill stands the Royal High School. Based on the Temple of Theseus in Athens it was designed by Thomas Hamilton in 1829. The school was converted into a debating chamber in 1976 but was deemed not suitable for the Scottish Parliament Building when devolution came to Scotland in 1999. It was decided the new building which can be seen in the foreground would be more fitting.

Edinburgh North Bridge
Viewed from Calton Hill

Edinburgh City
The Dugald Stewart Monument holds the commanding position atop Calton Hill.

Canongate and Arthur's Seat
From one vantage point to another, Calton Hill offers great views to Canongate and Holyrood Park.

St Andrew's House

On the southernmost slopes of Calton Hill,
St Andrew's House was completed in 1939
and is one of Scotland's finest Art Deco
buildings. The building houses the ministers
and staff of the Scottish Executive.

Edinburgh from Calton Hill

Snow is quite rare in Edinburgh, but certainly has a dramatic impact when it arrives.

Balmoral Clock, Edinburgh
Reminiscent of a time before wrist watches, the clock tower above the Balmoral Hotel has become one of Edinburgh's most famous landmarks.

The New Town - East to West

Edinburgh's New Town was designed by James Craig at just age 21. Following the draining of Nor Loch, now the site of Princes Street Gardens, the New Town was underway and within 30 years over 7,000 people from society's elite had made it their home. The symmetrical plan linked two gardened squares with an orderly grid work of straight and parallel streets.

Adorned with monuments and columns, the backbone of the New Town is George Street, named after King George III, it cemented a new era between Scotland and England.

Scottish National Portrait Gallery

LEFT *Running parallel to George Street, Queen Street's most striking building houses the Portrait Gallery. This neo-Gothic Victorian building with its arcaded entrance dates from the 1880s and is constructed from warm red sandstone.*

Royal Bank of Scotland

Building of the New Town began in 1767 from east to west with St Andrew Square, with its centrepiece as the Melville Monument (1821). Note also the domed roofed Dundas House (1773), a grand town house, now the headquarters of the Royal Bank of Scotland.

The Dome

ABOVE *A little way along George Street is The Dome, boasting a magnificent cupola roof this property was once a bank but is now an upmarket bistro. It is even more striking internally.*

Parish Church of St Andrew & St George

RIGHT *Built in 1784 as St Andrew's, the name changed to its present title when it was joined by the congregation from St George's Church in 1964 which is now West Register House.*

The Royal Society of Edinburgh, George Street

LEFT *Statue commemorating George IV's visit to Scotland in 1822, the first time a monarch had visited Scotland in over two centuries.*

Moray Place

RIGHT *Such was the demand, that the New Town continued to expand under the management of William Playfair, all be it on a less formal but still orderly and perhaps more elegant design of gardened crescents and circuses.*

The Georgian House, Charlotte Square

LEFT *Completing the western end of George Street and the pinnacle of Georgian architecture is Charlotte Square. Named after Queen Charlotte, wife of George III, the square was designed by Robert Adam in 1791. The property at No 7, The Georgian House, is cared for by the National Trust for Scotland and the interior depicts a typical home from the period.*

West Register House

Originally St George's Church, West Register House, another cupola roofed building stands at the western end of Charlotte Square. In the centre of the Square is an equestrian statue of Price Albert riding his horse, which pleased Queen Victoria so much that she immediately knighted the sculptor.

Edinburgh International Conference Centre

Internationally acclaimed, the Edinburgh International Conference Centre has won several architectural awards and has become the hub for Edinburgh's 'new' financial centre.

Edinburgh Castle from Castle Terrace

BELOW The huge and much needed barracks were added to the castle in 1796-9. Capable of housing an entire infantry battalion of 600, a garrison was stationed here until 1923.

St Mary's Episcopal Cathedral

LEFT *The cathedral's 10 bells were cast in 1878 although the building was not complete until the following year and the towers were not added until 1917. A typical Gothic structure and the largest to be built in Scotland following the Reformation, its central tower rises 84m.*

Beyond the Centre

Dean Village

RIGHT *A 'village within a city' and only a few minutes walk of the hustle and bustle of Edinburgh's centre lies secluded and serene Dean Village. Established during the 12th century in a 100ft deep gorge, this was a thriving community supporting 11 mills and 2 granaries, powered by the turbulent Water of Leith.*

Dean Gallery

LEFT *The fascinating cloud formation above the Dean Gallery is tribute to the art on display within the 19th century ex-hospital that was opened as an art gallery in 1999.*

Scottish National Gallery of Modern Art

BELOW LEFT *Scotland is famed for its links golf courses which are now artistically represented in the sculptured grounds around one of the city's 19th century neo-classical properties. A former school it is now being utilised as a modern art gallery.*

Fettes College

BELOW *Funded by successful merchant, Sir William Fettes, who left his wealth to fund a school after his only son died, aged 27, of typhoid. The imposing building with its gargoyles and towers is part Scottish Baronial and part French Loire. It took six years to complete and opened in 1870. Among its many successful and prominent students is Tony Blair, Prime Minister of Great Britain 1997-*

Royal Botanic Garden

Originally established next to the Palace of Holyroodhouse in 1670 by two physicians, the Royal Botanic Garden was relocated to its present 28ha (72 acres) site in 1823.

Not just a beautiful garden with over 16,000 species of plants for the publics enjoyment, it also continues to be a place of serious research.

Leith

Leith has been Edinburgh's sea port since the 14th century. A fiercely independent town until 1920, Leith was an industrial community, thriving when Britain was known for its ship building. With the decline of the shipping and heavy industries, Leith is now being radically redeveloped to support Britain's current high tech businesses and a new community of professionals paying high prices to live in the converted dockside warehousing.

Royal Yacht Britannia

After one million miles, 600 ports and the 4 royal honeymoons of Princesses Margaret and Ann, and Princes Charles and Edward, the Royal Yacht Britannia has ended its seafaring days. Launched in 1953, the ship provided an escape and sanctuary for the Royal Family but was decommissioned in 1997 and is now permanently moored along side Ocean Terminal in Leith. It is now a floating museum offering a nostalgic glimpse into the esteemed world in which the royal family, their servants, staff, guests and 260 officers and yachtsmen travelled.

Lauriston Castle

ABOVE *The tower of Lauriston Castle was built in the 16th century, with the adjoining mansion being added three centuries later. It remained in private ownership on the north-west outskirts of the city until very recently and maintains an interesting Edwardian interior.*

Craigmillar Castle

TOP RIGHT *South of the city and an excellent example of a medieval fortress, stands Cragmillar Castle. Despite being the location where the plotting of Lord Darnley, husband of Mary Queen of Scots, took place, it is here that the Queen sought safe haven following the murder of her secretary, Rizzio in 1566.*

Forth Bridge

Acclaimed the 'Eighth Wonder of the World', the Forth (Rail) Bridge is certainly an engineering masterpiece, spanning over 1 mile, it was the biggest bridge and an accolade for its time. Complete in 1890 it now looks extremely bulky and over-engineered compared to the equally impressive Forth Road Bridge built alongside it just 74 years later. 57 men lost their lives building the Forth Bridge which can expand up to 2m (7ft) in hot weather.

Index